JUST ME AND MOM

By: C Brutus

Hi, I'm Ben. I've been thinking a lot about something that's bothering me. At school, I see a lot of kids with both their moms and dads. They get picked up, their parents come to games, and they even bake cookies for parties. But for me, it's just my mom.

I love my mom. She's the best. She tells me funny stories before bed, helps me with my homework, and always makes sure we have pancakes on Saturday mornings. But lately, I've started to wonder about something, and I can't stop thinking about it.

One day, after school, I was sitting at the kitchen table while my mom cooked dinner. She had just come home from work, and she looked really tired. I watched her move around the kitchen, her eyes heavy, and I felt this question bubbling up inside me. I had to ask.

"Mom?" I said, fiddling with my fork. She turned around and smiled at me, even though she looked like she needed to lie down.

"Yes, Ben?"

I took a deep breath. "Why is it just us? Why don't I have a dad like the other kids?"

For a second, everything got quiet, like even the house was holding its breath. Mom put down the spoon she was using to stir the spaghetti sauce and came over to sit next to me. She took my hand, her smile a little sad now.

"That's a big question," she said softly. "I know you see other kids with two parents, and it makes you wonder. And that's okay, Ben."

I nodded. "Yeah. It's just... it feels different. Like, I only see you. You work so much, and you're always so tired. I don't know why things are like this."

Mom sighed and looked down at her hands for a moment before she spoke. "Every family is different, Ben. Some kids have a mom and a dad, some have just one parent, like you, and some live with grandparents or aunts and uncles. There are all kinds of families, and each one is special in its own way."

"But it's hard," I said. "I see you working all the time, and sometimes I wish you didn't have to work so much. I wish I had someone else here to help you."

Mom squeezed my hand. "I know, sweetie. I do work a lot, and sometimes it's really hard. But I work because I want to make sure we have everything we need. I want you to have a good life, and I'm doing everything I can to make that happen."

I thought about the times I'd see her come home late; her face tired but still smiling at me. I thought about how sometimes she couldn't come to school events because she had to work. It made me feel sad, even though I knew she loved me.

"I just wish you weren't so tired all the time," I whispered.

Mom looked at me, her eyes a little shiny like she was about to cry, but she didn't. Instead, she pulled me into a hug. "Even when I'm tired, Ben, being with you is the best part of my day. You're my whole world, and I wouldn't trade that for anything."

Her words made me feel warm inside, like everything would be okay. But I still had one more question. "Mom, do you ever get sad? Because it's just us?"

She paused, like she was thinking hard. "Sometimes," she admitted. "Sometimes it's hard, and I do wish I had more help. But you know what? You make it all worth it. Every smile, every laugh, every hug—those are the things that keep me going. You make our little family complete."

Hearing that made me feel a little better. I still wished things were different sometimes, but maybe our family was just the way it was meant to be. And even if it was just me and Mom, that didn't mean we weren't a real family.

I hugged her tight, and as we sat there together, I realized something important: even if it was just the two of us, we had all the love we needed.

And that was enough.

Dear Readers,

I want to take a moment to express my deepest gratitude to each of you. Whether you've just started reading my books or have been with me from the beginning, your support means the world to me. Writing is a journey that comes to life when readers like you engage with the words, stories, and characters I create.

Your encouragement, feedback, and enthusiasm inspire me every day to continue doing what I love. Thank you for allowing my books to be a part of your life and for joining me on this adventure.

With heartfelt appreciation,

C Brutus